IRELAND BY RAIL

THE NATIONAL RAILWAY MUSEUM, YORK
A BOOK OF POSTCARDS

Pomegranate

SAN FRANCISCO

Pomegranate Communications, Inc.
Box 808022, Petaluma CA 94975
800 227 1428; www.pomegranate.com

Pomegranate Europe Ltd.
Unit 1, Heathcote Business Centre, Hurlbutt Road
Warwick, Warwickshire CV34 6TD, UK
[+44] 0 1926 430111; sales@pomeurope.co.uk

ISBN 978-0-7649-5984-4
Pomegranate Catalog No. AA685

Pomegranate publishes books of postcards on a wide range of subjects.
Please contact the publisher for more information.

Cover designed by Patrice Morris
Printed in Korea
20 19 18 17 16 15 14 13 12 11   10 9 8 7 6 5 4 3 2 1

To facilitate detachment of the postcards from this book, fold each card along its perforation line before tearing.

These were hard times for Ireland. During the 1920s and 1930s a global depression and foreign competition brought unemployment to many regions. At the same time, railway companies were struggling to compete with trucking firms and private automobiles. Great Britain's major railways enlisted the help of artists to create for them alluring, alternative visions to the stark, modernizing world.

Featuring rolling hillsides, glimmering streams, uncrowded seashores, and dramatic mountain vistas, the advertising posters functioned as colorful, oversized snapshots, perhaps focused from the rolling luxury of a railway car. The trains themselves were seldom featured; instead the artists portrayed the idyllic countryside and historic sites to entice potential passengers to purchase tickets for the privilege of taking in such wonders with their own eyes.

The thirty postcards in this book were selected from the collections of the National Railway Museum, York, the largest railway museum in the world. Its permanent displays and collections illustrate over 200 years of British railway history from the Industrial Revolution to the present day. The NRM includes a fabulous collection of railway advertising posters charting the history of rail.

GREAT WESTERN RAILWAY

WARWICK GOBLE

SOUTHERN IRELAND

Free illustrated booklet obtainable
at G.W.R. Stations and Offices

Ireland by Rail

Warwick Goble (English, 1862–1943)
Southern Ireland

Great Western Railway poster
Collection of the National Railway Museum, York

707 782 9000   WWW.POMEGRANATE.COM

Pomegranate

BY NORMAN WILKINSON, R.I.

BELFAST LOUGH -- THE GATEWAY TO HAPPY HOLIDAYS
COME TO ULSTER

Travel by the Royal Mail Routes via Heysham, Liverpool or Stranraer.   Express Services and Cheap Fares

INFORMATION REGARDING ULSTER AND FREE ILLUSTRATED GUIDE CAN BE HAD ON APPLICATION TO THE
ULSTER TOURIST DEVELOPMENT ASSOCIATION LTD., DEPT. 3, 6 ROYAL AVENUE, BELFAST

Ireland by Rail

Norman Wilkinson (1878-1971)
Come to Ulster, c. 1930s

London, Midland & Scottish Railway poster
Collection of the National Railway Museum, York

707 782 9000 WWW.POMEGRANATE.COM

Pomegranate

L M S

LONDON MIDLAND & SCOTTISH RAILWAY

CONNEMARA

BY PAUL HENRY

"IRELAND THIS YEAR"

Ireland by Rail

Paul Henry (Irish, 1876–1958)
Connemara, 1923–1947

London, Midland & Scottish Railway poster
Collection of the National Railway Museum, York

707 782 9000 WWW.POMEGRANATE.COM

Pomegranate

SOUTHERN IRELAND

TRAVEL IN COMFORT BY RAIL AND

BRITISH RAILWAYS

IRELAND BY RAIL

Jack Merriott (English, 1901–1968)
Southern Ireland, 1948–1965

British Railways (Western Region) poster
Collection of the National Railway Museum, York

707 782 9000   WWW.POMEGRANATE.COM

Pomegranate

THE GIANT'S CAUSEWAY
by Norman Wilkinson, P.R.I.

IRELAND
FOR HOLIDAYS

LONDON MIDLAND AND SCOTTISH RAILWAY

IRELAND BY RAIL

Norman Wilkinson (English, 1878–1971)
Ireland for Holidays—The Giant's Causeway, 1923–1947

London, Midland & Scottish Railway poster
Collection of the National Railway Museum, York

WWW.POMEGRANATE.COM   707 782 9000

Pomegranate

IRELAND OVERNIGHT

DUBLIN via Holyhead | **BELFAST** via Heysham

For Dublin reservations apply to
District Marine Manager, Holyhead, Anglesey

BRITISH RAILWAYS

For Belfast reservations apply to
District Marine Manager, Heysham Harbour, Lancs.

IRELAND BY RAIL

Claude Buckle (English, 1905–1973)
Ireland Overnight—Dublin via Holyhead / Belfast via Heysham

British Railways (London Midland Region) poster
Collection of the National Railway Museum, York

707 782 9000   WWW.POMEGRANATE.COM

Pomegranate

LMS

LONDON MIDLAND & SCOTTISH RAILWAY

BY NORMAN WILKINSON R.I.

ROCK OF CASHEL

IRELAND FOR HOLIDAYS

IRELAND BY RAIL

Norman Wilkinson (English, 1878–1971)
Ireland for Holidays—Rock of Cashel, c. 1930s

London, Midland & Scottish Railway poster
Collection of the National Railway Museum, York

707 782 9000 WWW.POMEGRANATE.COM

Pomegranate

KILLARNEY

IRELAND
FOR HOLIDAYS

LONDON MIDLAND AND SCOTTISH RAILWAY

Holiday Contract Tickets, 10/- Third Class, 15/- First Class, are available in this District during the Holiday Season

Ireland by Rail

Clodagh Sparrow (active 1930s)
Ireland for Holidays—Killarney, c. 1930s

London, Midland & Scottish Railway poster
Collection of the National Railway Museum, York

707 782 9000   WWW.POMEGRANATE.COM

Pomegranate

MEETING OF THE WATERS

KILLARNEY
TRAVEL VIA FISHGUARD — THE DIRECT ROUTE

IRELAND BY RAIL

Leonard Richmond (English, 1889–1965)
Killarney, 1938

Great Western Railway poster
Collection of the National Railway Museum, York

707 782 9000   WWW.POMEGRANATE.COM

Pomegranate

—NORMAN WILKINSON

THE ANTRIM COAST ROAD

By NORMAN WILKINSON, P.R.I.

IRELAND
for HOLIDAYS

LONDON MIDLAND AND SCOTTISH RAILWAY

Seven day Holiday Zone Tickets. 10/- Third Class. 13/- Second Class and 20/- First Class, are available in this District during the Holiday Season

Ireland by Rail

Norman Wilkinson (English, 1878–1971)
Ireland for Holidays—The Antrim Coast Road, 1923–1947

London, Midland & Scottish Railway poster
Collection of the National Railway Museum, York

707 782 9000   WWW.POMEGRANATE.COM

Pomegranate

IRELAND BY RAIL

Artist unknown
Ireland by LMS—The Royal Mail Routes, 1935

London, Midland & Scottish Railway poster
Collection of the National Railway Museum, York

707 782 9000   WWW.POMEGRANATE.COM

Pomegranate

MIDLAND STATION HOTEL

BELFAST

an L M S HOTEL
(NORTHERN COUNTIES COMMITTEE)

FOR TARIFF PARTICULARS APPLY TO RESIDENT MANAGER.

Ireland by Rail

Gordon Nicoll (English, 1888–1959)
Midland Station Hotel, Belfast, 1923–1947

London, Midland & Scottish Railway poster
Collection of the National Railway Museum, York

707 782 9000   WWW.POMEGRANATE.COM

Pomegranate

GLENARIFF
By Norman Wilkinson, R.I.

LMS

Of all the lovely Antrim glens, Glenariff is queen. From Parkmore the stream drops by a long series of beautiful cascades, richly embowered in vivid foliage, down to the bottom of the glen, close to Cushendall on the shores of Red Bay. As the glen widens, a superb view over the Irish Sea opens out, with Kintyre, Ailsa Craig and the Lowlands of Galloway standing out on the horizon. Visit Northern Ireland by the Royal Mail Routes (Heysham, Liverpool or Stranraer), thence to Glenariff by L M S rail and motor, or motor only, almost 100 miles through fresh and unspoilt countryside and along the famous Antrim Coast Road.

IRELAND BY RAIL

Norman Wilkinson (English, 1878–1971)
Glenariff, 1923–1947

London, Midland & Scottish Railway poster
Collection of the National Railway Museum, York

707 782 9000   WWW.POMEGRANATE.COM

Pomegranate

BANGOR
NORTHERN IRELAND

ILLUSTRATED GUIDE FREE FROM PUBLICITY MANAGER, THE CASTLE, BANGOR, NORTHERN IRELAND
TRAIN AND STEAMER SERVICES AND FARES FROM STATIONS, OFFICES AND AGENCIES

BRITISH RAILWAYS

IRELAND BY RAIL

A. J. Wilson (b. 1924)
Bangor, 1955

British Railways (London Midland Region) poster
Collection of the National Railway Museum, York

707 782 9000   WWW.POMEGRANATE.COM

Pomegranate

PORTRUSH
NORTHERN IRELAND

ILLUSTRATED GUIDE FREE
FROM INFORMATION BUREAU,
DEPT. BR. PORTRUSH

BRITISH RAILWAYS

TRAIN AND STEAMER
SERVICES AND FARES FROM
STATIONS AND AGENCIES

IRELAND BY RAIL

Lance Cattermole (Irish, 1898–1992)
Portrush, 1952

British Railways (London Midland Region) poster
Collection of the National Railway Museum, York

707 782 9000   WWW.POMEGRANATE.COM

Pomegranate

LMS

GOLF IN NORTHERN IRELAND
THE 8TH GREEN AT PORTRUSH
by
NORMAN WILKINSON, R.I.

IRELAND BY RAIL

Norman Wilkinson (English, 1878–1971)
Golf in Northern Ireland, c. 1925

London, Midland & Scottish Railway poster
Collection of the National Railway Museum, York

707 782 9000   WWW.POMEGRANATE.COM

Pomegranate

IRELAND BY RAIL

Artist unknown
The North-West of Ireland, c. 1930s

Donegal Railway Company poster
Collection of the National Railway Museum, York

707 782 9000   WWW.POMEGRANATE.COM

Pomegranate

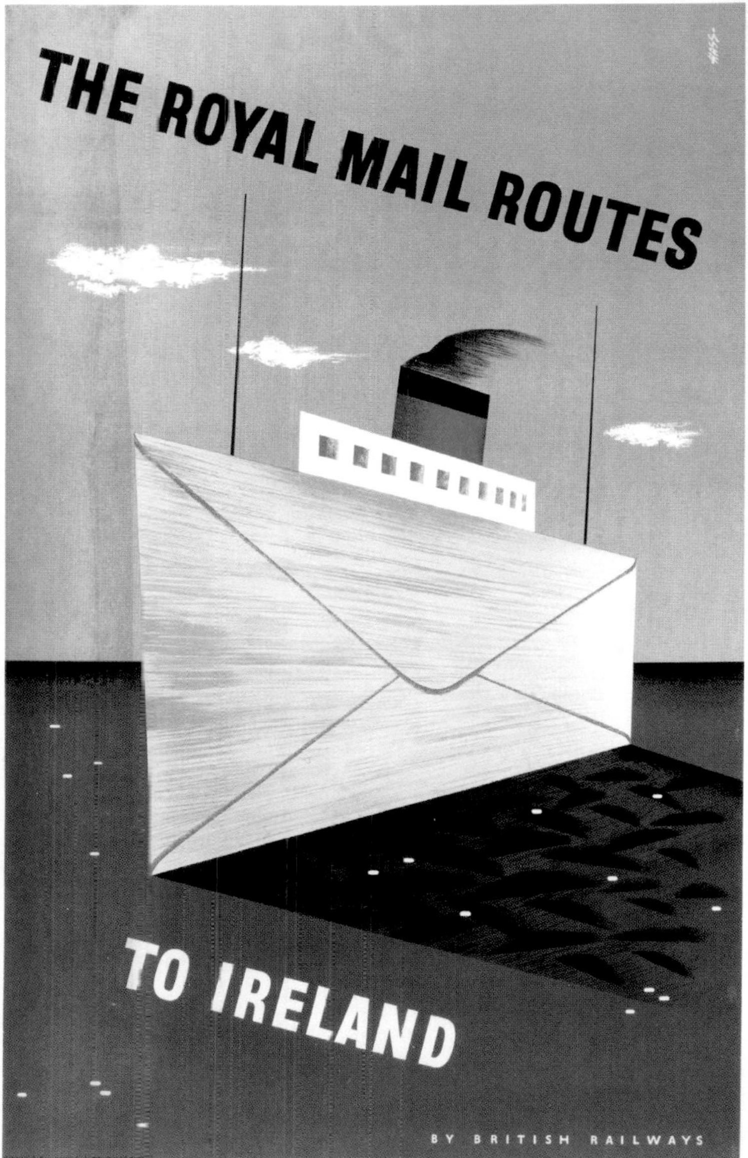
THE ROYAL MAIL ROUTES
TO IRELAND
BY BRITISH RAILWAYS

IRELAND BY RAIL

Hass (active 1952)
The Royal Mail Routes to Ireland, 1952

British Railways (London Midland Region) poster
Collection of the National Railway Museum, York

707 782 9000   WWW.POMEGRANATE.COM

Pomegranate

- NORMAN WILKINSON -

GREENISLAND VIADUCTS
COUNTY ANTRIM, NORTHERN IRELAND
by NORMAN WILKINSON R.I.

LMS

The Greenisland Loop Line on the Northern Counties Committee, opened in 1934, was constructed to obviate the necessity of trains to and from Belfast and Stations in the North running via Greenisland. The new line is approximately three miles in length and has a continuous gradient of 1 in 75. The Main Line Viaduct which is the largest reinforced concrete railway viaduct in the British Isles, is 630 feet long and has a maximum height of 70 feet above the level of the stream. The Main Arches in the Main Line and Down Shore Line Viaducts have a span of 89 feet. Over 32,000 tons of concrete, reinforced with 700 tons of steel, were required for the construction of the two viaducts.

IRELAND BY RAIL

Norman Wilkinson (English, 1878–1971)
Greenisland Viaducts, 1923–1947

London, Midland & Scottish Railway poster
Collection of the National Railway Museum, York

707 782 9000 WWW.POMEGRANATE.COM

Pomegranate

PAUL HENRY

LOUGH DERG

IRELAND *for* **HOLIDAYS**

BRITISH RAILWAYS

IRELAND BY RAIL

Paul Henry (Irish, 1876–1958)
Lough Derg—Ireland for Holidays, c. 1949

British Railways (London Midland Region) poster
Collection of the National Railway Museum, York

707 782 9000   WWW.POMEGRANATE.COM

Pomegranate

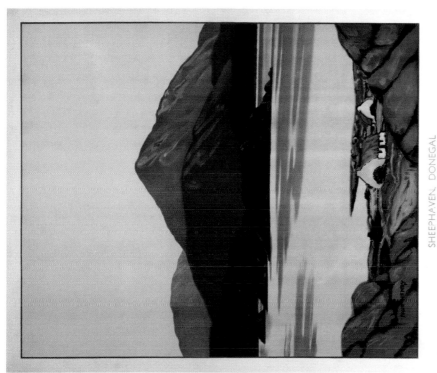

SHEEPHAVEN, DONEGAL

TO IRELAND WITH EASE
BY RAIL AND SEA

RESERVED SEATS · RESTAURANT CARS BY DAY
SLEEPING CARS BY NIGHT · FAST NEW VESSELS
WITH LUXURY CABINS AND LOUNGES

BRITISH RAILWAYS

BRITISH & IRISH STEAMSHIP
COMPANY LTD.

BELFAST STEAMSHIP
COMPANY LTD.

IRELAND BY RAIL

Paul Henry (Irish, 1876–1958)
To Ireland with Ease by Rail and Sea—Sheephaven, Donegal, 1951

British Railways (London Midland Region) poster in conjunction with the British & Irish Steamship Company Ltd. and the Belfast Steamship Company Ltd.
Collection of the National Railway Museum, York

707 782 9000 WWW.POMEGRANATE.COM

Pomegranate

IRISH MAIL 1848-1948

The Irish Mail ranks as one of the most famous of British Railways' expresses, and as the oldest named train in the world. In this poster first published in 1937 and re-issued in August 1948, to commemorate the centenary of the Irish Mail route to Ireland via Holyhead and Dun Laoghaire (Kingstown), the train is shewn leaving Robert Stephenson's mighty Tubular Bridge over the Menai Strait

A CENTURY OF SERVICE

BRITISH RAILWAYS

F.H Glazebrook

IRELAND BY RAIL

F. H. Glazebrook
Irish Mail, 1948

British Railways poster
Collection of the National Railway Museum, York

707 782 9000   WWW.POMEGRANATE.COM

Pomegranate

NORTHERN COUNTIES HOTEL
PORTRUSH
NORTHERN IRELAND
an LMS HOTEL
(NORTHERN COUNTIES COMMITTEE)
FOR TARIFF PARTICULARS APPLY TO RESIDENT MANAGER

IRELAND BY RAIL

Gordon Nicoll (English, 1888–1959)
Northern Counties Hotel, Portrush, 1923–1947

London, Midland & Scottish Railway poster
Collection of the National Railway Museum, York

707 782 9000   WWW.POMEGRANATE.COM

Pomegranate

SHEEPHAVEN
By NORMAN WILKINSON R.I.

DONEGAL
FOR HOLIDAYS

LONDON MIDLAND AND SCOTTISH RAILWAY

IRELAND BY RAIL

Norman Wilkinson (English, 1878–1971)
Donegal for Holidays, 1923–1947

London, Midland & Scottish Railway poster
Collection of the National Railway Museum, York

707 782 9000   WWW.POMEGRANATE.COM

Pomegranate

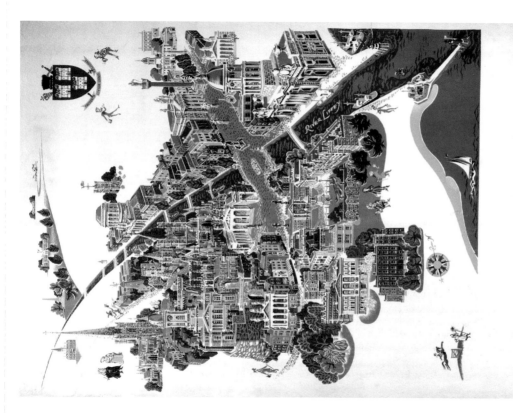

DUBLIN

Travel there in comfort by rail and sea

BRITISH RAILWAYS

IRELAND BY RAIL

Kerry Lee (active 1950s)
Dublin, 1954

British Railways poster
Collection of the National Railway Museum, York

707 782 9000   WWW.POMEGRANATE.COM

Pomegranate

LMS

SPORT ON THE LMS
IRELAND VIA HOLYHEAD

NORMAN WILKINSON, R.I.

IRELAND BY RAIL

Norman Wilkinson (English, 1878–1971)
Sport on the LMS—Ireland via Holyhead, c. 1930s

London, Midland & Scottish Railway poster
Collection of the National Railway Museum, York

707 782 9000   WWW.POMEGRANATE.COM

Pomegranate

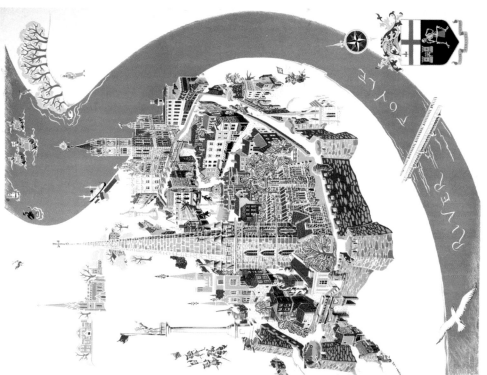

LONDONDERRY

Travel there in comfort by rail and sea

RIVER FOYLE

BRITISH RAILWAYS

IRELAND BY RAIL

Kerry Lee (active 1950s)
Londonderry, 1953

British Railways poster
Collection of the National Railway Museum, York

707 782 9000   WWW.POMEGRANATE.COM

Pomegranate

TRAVEL TO IRELAND BY
THE SHORT SEA ROUTE

STRANRAER-LARNE

**MAGNIFICENT NEW TURBINE STEAMERS
'PRINCESS MAUD' AND 'PRINCESS MARGARET'**

GREATLY ACCELERATED SERVICES

PARTICULARS OF TRAIN AND STEAMER TIMES FROM
ANY L M S STATION

IRELAND BY RAIL

Norman Wilkinson (English, 1878–1971)
Stranraer–Larne, Magnificent New Turbine Steamers
'Princess Maud' and 'Princess Margaret,' c. 1930s

London, Midland & Scottish Railway poster
Collection of the National Railway Museum, York

707 782 9000 WWW.POMEGRANATE.COM

Pomegranate

LAUNCH of T.S.S. DUKE of YORK
QUEEN'S ISLAND, BELFAST
painted by Norman Wilkinson R.I.

LMS

The new LMS steamer "Duke of York" built by Messrs. Harland & Wolff Ltd, Belfast, was launched on the 7th March, 1935, by the Duchess of Abercorn. The steamer is for the Heysham-Belfast Service and has restaurants, smoke rooms and lounges for both First and Third Class passengers. The "Duke of York" is equipped with mechanical stokers, and an automatic sprinkler and fire alarm system is fitted throughout the passenger accommodation. The dimensions of the ship are:—
Overall length 349 ft.   Breadth 52 ft.   Depth 19 ft. 6 ins.   and has a speed of 21 knots.

IRELAND BY RAIL

Norman Wilkinson (English, 1878–1971)
Launch of the T.S.S. Duke of York, 1935

London, Midland & Scottish Railway poster
Collection of the National Railway Museum, York

707 782 9000   WWW.POMEGRANATE.COM

Pomegranate

Ireland by Rail

Leonard Cusden
Fishguard–Rosslare, 1932

Great Western Railway poster
Collection of the National Railway Museum, York

707 782 9000   WWW.POMEGRANATE.COM

Pomegranate